William Morgan

'God's Word for Wales'

NATHAN MUNDAY

Er cof am Tadcu

Contents

List of Illustrations

Acknowledgement

The photographs of William Morgan, the Drovers, Sir John Wynn, Richard Vaughan and John Whitgift, and *Y Drych Cristianogawl* are reproduced by kind permission of the National Library of Wales, Aberystwyth.

Series Preface

Mission and Vision: Welsh greats who changed the world for Christ is a series of very readable short biographies of men and women from Wales who have had an amazing influence for good.

Whatever your age or wherever you come from, it is hoped that these real-life stories will inspire you to delve more deeply into their lives. They are meant to excite younger people as well as older readers to take an interest in history and especially in individuals who are so little remembered or even neglected but who have made a significant impact not only in Wales but more generally throughout Britain and beyond.

It is our earnest prayer that the Lord would use these biographical sketches to stimulate, encourage and challenge those who read them to live to the glory of God and the advancement of his kingdom.

Philip H Eveson
Chairman of the Bryntirion Press Committee

William Morgan Timeline

1374	Death of Petrarch
1384	Death of John Wycliffe
1509	Birth of John Calvin
1516	Erasmus's New Testament is published
1517	Luther nails the 95 theses to the Castle Church door
1520	William Salesbury is born
c.1545	William Morgan is born
1546	Martin Luther dies
1547	Edward VI ascends the throne on the death of his father, Henry VIII
1553	Mary I ('Bloody Mary') becomes queen
c.1555	William Morgan goes to Gwydir Castle
1558	Elizabeth I ascends the throne on the death of her half-sister Mary
1564	Death of John Calvin
c.1565	Tŷ Mawr is refurbished and William begins his studies at Cambridge University
1567	Salesbury's New Testament is published
1568	William ordained at Ely Cathedral
1572-5	Llanbadarn Fawr
1575-8	Welshpool
1578-95	Llanrhaeadr-ym-Mochnant
1588	The Welsh Bible is published in London
1588	The Spanish Armada
1595	Bishop of Llandaff
1601	Bishop of St Asaph
1603	Elizabeth I dies. James VI of Scotland becomes James I of England
1604	William dies at the age of 59
1604	Hampton Court Conference
1611	King James Bible is published
1620	The Revision of the Welsh Bible by Davies and Parry is published

Introduction: Wybrnant 2019

I t was raining. We were driving towards a remote valley in the heart of the Snowdonian foothills. The landscape was bare. The browns, greys and blacks were sometimes dotted with white blobs; the terrain-disturbers turned out to be sheep. The poor creatures leapt off the banks and disappeared into the mist. My wife sighed with relief when she realized that the helpless flock had not fallen to their deaths but were squatting rather happily in the shadow of a rock. The rain was like percussion. I looked at my wife; she looked at me. I started to think what on earth we were doing in such an unfamiliar place.

As the mist lifted, the countryside presented itself. We followed its flow with our eyes as it rolled down towards the river Machno. Farmhouses formed in the clouds while a vacant square chapel stared at us like a sentinel. These buildings were both encouraging and discouraging. On the one hand, the farms indicated that we were not that far removed from civilization. The mist had been playing tricks on us. On the other hand, a deep sadness filled me as I observed the old relic from our Nonconformist past. Wales may be an ancient landscape but these monuments seem prematurely vacant. Now, they are extra items added to that mental inventory which makes an area Welsh. The dry-stone walls and snaking roads informed my Dutch wife that she was a very long way from her homeland. Such characteristics have provided a kind of hallmark for this area for centuries.

We entered the village of Penmachno. After some narrow turns through the village, we ascended a steep road bordered by a dark woodland. The memory of civilization soon faded as we entered the realm of badger and buzzard. We were intruding outsiders. Having reached the brow of the hill, a high grassland emerged on the right. Some Welsh ponies stood by the fence greeting us as we drove by. A brown sign with an oak leaf encouraged us towards our destination. It had 'Tŷ Mawr' written on it.

You may be thinking how on earth is this modern car journey linked to the subject of this small book? Well, the place that we were heading for was 'Tŷ Mawr' ('Great House'). It's a special house because it is the birthplace of Bible translator, William Morgan (c.1545-1604). I had accepted the job of warden of his first home. I would also be a keeper of many books, or rather, Bibles, which makes this special place a library in the wilderness. The most important book under my care is one of the last copies of the 1588 translation of the Welsh Bible, Morgan's masterpiece.

He was not born in a palace or an academic hub. He did not begin his life speaking many languages. Nor did he have that infamous 'Moses beard', as one schoolchild put it when I first began as warden. Thomas Prytherch's 1907 portrait is the most well-known image we have of Morgan. Moses remains a good comparison. Both have been portrayed as lawgivers, saviours, prophets and heroes. The image captures him in his bishop's garb: black hat, white cassock and Tudor sleeves. And then, the eye is drawn to the Bible which, if

William Morgan

you squint your eyes, he is handing out to you, the observer. That child was on to something.

From now on, my day-to-day job would be to share Morgan's story. I tell visitors about the bearded man and how his translation not only saved the Welsh language but also meant that the words of eternal life (John 6:68) became available to his fellow countrymen in their own language.

Having reached the end of the pine forest, the road opened and presented us with a spectacular view. I could see our future life tucked in the corner of the valley, with some farm buildings, an enclosed garden, a stone bridge, a bubbling stream and a woodshed. A farm gate had to be opened before we continued down the road. We drove down and noticed various pigs patrolling the fields we passed. At the valley floor, we parked outside the small enclosure. We walked through a stiff, small gate and saw a little avenue of fruit trees and stepping-stones. On our left, Tŷ Mawr sat in the middle of the lawn like an old man, centuries old. The first thing we noticed were its chimneys: one straight and the other bent like a stiff back. We also noticed that it was not that big at all. In fact, it blended rather well with the other rocky outcrops which adorn the high valley. The masonry looked well-weathered and a mossy slate plaque above the door read (in translation):

Tŷ Mawr
Wybrnant
Here was born in 1545
Wm. Morgan D.D., Bishop of St Asaph
The first translator
Of the complete Bible into Welsh
He died September 10th 1604
Restored 1988

Plaque on Tŷ Mawr

An iconic stone bridge crossed the stream. Toilet block, exhibition room and a woodshed – these outbuildings lead to a small cottage which is where we now live. *Glan yr Afon* used to be the Tŷ Mawr's pigsty. It was refurbished in the late 1980s to house the warden's family while Tŷ Mawr was changed from farmhouse to museum. It is now as it would have been in the 1560s.

There is some debate about the meaning of the 'Wybrnant'. Some say that it denotes 'a stream laden with mist', or 'the stream flowing from the sky'. My favourite definition is 'the adder or dragon's stream'. Menacing! Yes, but it is beautiful to walk along its bank during the autumn months and even better when the tiny trout leap in the spring. The stream provides us with fresh water, which is pumped directly into the house and, more recently, a new micro-hydro system has been installed so that the current is also used to create electricity for the houses.

Tŷ Mawr

My aim in this small book is to introduce you to William Morgan and document the vision that eventually provided the Welsh people with their Bible. As with any historical figure from this period, we cannot know every single detail concerning his or her life. This book does not always function as an accurate historical record, but it seeks to capture some of the more important facts whilst employing the imagination at times in order to fill in the gaps.

I want to begin by taking an imaginary tour of his first home. This is the kind of tour people receive when they come to the house itself. It will not only place you in the present house, but will also take you back in time and explain how the house has changed. Through living at Wybrnant, I have become convinced that William's upbringing was an important time of preparation for what he was destined to achieve later in his life. After this, we will leave Tŷ Mawr and follow William on his travels. Morgan was not the first man to be inspired by the hope of providing his people with God's word in their own language, nor would he be the last. However, he was the most important factor in making the *Beibl Cysegr-Lan* available, firstly, in Welsh pulpits, and subsequently, in Welsh hands. It is a journey which involves many characters, numerous cities, and an exciting history which, I hope, will encourage you to delve deeper into William Morgan's story.

We begin with the house which witnessed the birth of Wales's most important Bible translator.

Chapter 1: The Translator's Nursery

Welcome to Tŷ Mawr, Wybrnant – the translator's nursery. This is not where the Bible was translated but it was an important preparatory ground for young William. The house sits in a high valley and has been in the care of the National Trust since 1951. Let's take a closer look at this unique nursery.

Back in Tudor Wales, farms were quite small; they were usually only of 15 to 30 acres. Each farmer in the parish, however, had rights of common pasture for as many cattle as he could winter on his farm. The bolder farmers were already enclosing the common grazing around the villages. Most rural houses like this one were single-storey and white-washed. You may already be familiar with the idea of a *tŷ hir Cymreig* ('long Welsh farmhouse'); this is how Tŷ Mawr was designed. Before we proceed through the door, let's turn around and look at the valley again.

Outside

Back in the sixteenth century, this was a much busier valley than it appears today. Tŷ Mawr was situated on a relatively well-used drover's road; to be more precise, the house sat on a kind of crossroads – the river being the parish boundary. We should imagine travellers coming and going; some of them would even have stopped in this place for some rest.

Who were these drovers? They were a kind of nomadic farmer who moved sheep, cattle, and geese. Yet they also 'moved' money, language, dialect, accent, hangers-on, men, women, children and dogs. Imagine the noise! Some historians suggest that the geese wore leather shoes to preserve their little feet on the long journey. And they did have a long journey. Many of them would have travelled all the way to Smithfield Market in London. Wales is usually associated with sheep farming but, back then, cattle would have been the mainstay of the agricultural economy.

Perhaps you now have a picture of Tŷ Mawr as less of a farmhouse and more like an important hub, attracting all manner of life. It is a translator's nursery. The modern equivalent might be more of a motorway service station or a Travelodge! The drovers would come, tired and thirsty, via the high road from Dolwyddelan with its tall castle. Imagine one of the younger men suddenly noticing a distinct silhouette against the setting sun: Scots Pines.

'Look! The pines!' he would shout.

'Where?'

'There! Just above that smallholding!'

'Ah … we must be nearing Tŷ Mawr,' the older one would say. 'There'll be a good welcome for us there. We can graze for a few days.'

This would have been their conversation once they had spotted the trees. They knew that a cluster of Scots Pines above a smallholding meant there was a welcome. It was a sign of refreshment and a sign of goodwill. These ancient symbols have long been forgotten but, back then, the trees acted like the flashing motel signs on the side of our motorways. Drovers from the north of Wales brought pine cones down with them into England and planted them in clumps of three or five near the inns they wanted to recommend. If this was the case, it seems that Tŷ Mawr was highly recommended as a stopping point. Sadly, most of the old trees have long disappeared. Having descended into the grassy harbour, the drovers would soon be welcomed by the Morgans. They may well have taken some of the family's own cattle to market.

The photograph here was taken in the year 1885 in Montgomeryshire. By then around 30,000 cattle and sheep were

Nineteenth century drovers

driven from Wales to London each year. This was an ancient tradition that stretched well before William's time and was only eclipsed when the railways appeared. During Edward VI's reign, an act was passed to safeguard his subjects' herds and money, which meant that every drover had to be licensed by the district court or Quarter Sessions, proving that they were of 'good character, married, householders and over thirty years of age'. They were trustworthy folk. Look at the picture. They are hardy men. Their shoes are dusty and worn. The man on the right has a good coat because he would have often faced miserable weather, and the man on the left looks exhausted.

Inside

Now, we enter the house. The name of the house suggests that it was the most important farmstead in the valley. The entrance is low because people in Tudor times were much shorter than we are today. It will take some time for your eyes to adjust to the darkness. This entrance would once have been the centre of a long Welsh farmhouse erected around 1520. Two fragments of cruck trusses embedded in the east wall and the lower parts of the stone wall are all that remains of the original hall-house belonging to the Morgans. There may have been a crude crucifix attached to the doorpost. The family would have crossed themselves as they crossed the threshold. At that time, a very young King Henry VIII was on the throne, whilst Martin Luther was busy writing during the first pivotal years of the Reformation in Germany. God was already at work in this great continent.

The house would have been bustling. The area you have just entered would have been a service area – a kind of outdoor space connected to the interior. Imagine the dirty straw covering the floor. Some herbs may have been spread across the floor in order to repel the flies and provide a masking aroma – a very rustic 'potpourri'. The animals would not have been far away. They were neighbours, literally! This service area may have witnessed the cow being milked, or have sheltered the smaller livestock during the harsh winters. On your right you can see some doors which lead to two separate storage rooms and to your left the entrance to the main hall – the strategic heart of the house.

Today, a fire is burning at the far end of the wall. Its flames illuminate the beams on the ceiling which, if we follow each one, leads our gaze towards the biggest of them all, the Bressumer Beam situated above the hearth, dating back to 1565. However, it might surprise you to learn that this rustic room would have been unfamiliar to the young William. There wouldn't have been such a large hearth or the additional floor. The early modern furniture is not original to the house either. We need to use our imagination again to enter the hall of 1545 – the year that William Morgan was born.

It is smoky. Light is minimal and the smell of the food is vaguely familiar to you. Herbs have been scattered on the floor; they crunch as you progress towards the window. A mother nurses her baby in the corner. Her name is Lowri Wiliam, William's mother. The father, John ap Morgan, is smoking a clay pipe by the fireside. The fire isn't in a hearth, but positioned in the centre of the room on a stone platform a few inches off the floor. A large cast-iron cauldron is rocking gently over its flames. No chimney. Just a hole in the thatched roof allows some smoke to escape. The Morgans will try and keep some of it in the room. Sixteenth century families believed that smoke provided warmth as well as assisting the strewn herbs in their continual battle with insects. A large chest is in one of the corners, used to store clothes and foodstuffs. Rolled-up beds lean against the wall. In one sense, this main hall is an 'everything room' – sleeping, eating, talking, living.

What about food? There would be pottage for breakfast and supper, lots of oatmeal and fish but meat would have been a rare treat. An array of familiar and unfamiliar vegetables would have been available, but no potatoes, which had not yet reached the north of Wales. Oats and rye were grown in nearby fields, and it is likely that fish from the rivers would have provided the family with the bulk of their protein. One of the few documents that have survived from William's father is his fishing licence. Water or home-brewed beer would have been the beverages on offer.

William's parents were not peasants. On his father's side, he could trace a distinguished ancestry back to two of the original founders of the Fifteen Tribes of Gwynedd: Hedd 'Molwynog' and Nefydd Hardd. On his maternal side, he could trace his ancestry back to another one of those founders: Marchudd ap Cynan. However, by the time of William's birth, they had become 'servants to the house of Gwydir' – a connection which would later be very important for William's advancement. Gwydir Castle is very near to Llanrwst and can still be visited today. John and Lowri had five children. William was their second son. Unfortunately, we know hardly anything about his brother and sisters.

His father was a moderately prosperous tenant farmer on the Gwydir estate of the Wynn family. Some even argue that John ap Morgan was the chief steward of the estate – a kind of estate manager. His duties would have been tax-collecting and managing the forests and rivers. But most of his time would have been spent farming. It is likely that William would have had a good upbringing. To begin with, he would have heard so much as a child. A large part of North Wales would have been monolingual: only the Welsh language being spoken. The drovers and travellers that stayed in his valley came from all over the country. This meant of course, that they would also have brought their different accents and dialects into this small pocket of Wales. William would probably have heard and mastered the first of his many new languages at Wybrnant: English. There was no 'Duolingo' back then! Languages were learnt the good old-fashioned way by talking and listening to one another. He would also have had ample opportunities to hear the Welsh poets as they travelled through the area.

Today, the house has an upstairs where visitors may enter the famous Bible room which houses an original copy of the 1588 translation. It is kept in a regulated atmosphere in the kind of cabinet that you see in grander museums. Its pages are tattered by age, but its condition is relatively good for an object in its fifth century. Visitors can only see one 'original' page at a time but downstairs a facsimile (a perfect copy) allows those who wish, to look at it in its entirety.

As William grew, less time would have been spent inside. The general rule in this period was that the women stayed in the house and the men would be out in the fields or up on the hills. We know that he probably helped with his father's livestock. It was the practice in medieval times for whole families to live in a cabin in the hills during the summer months so as to tend their flocks and herds. William may have been accustomed to this tradition and have spent nights on the open mountain. In Wales, such a cabin was called the *hafod*. The animals' milk was made into butter and cheese on the hillside before bringing it downhill to be stored for the winter months or to sell in the nearby market of Llanrwst. If William did spend time in the *hafod*, he would have seen wonderful night skies and experienced the extreme weather conditions which frequently batter the high valley.

It's not going too far to suggest that the natural landscape surrounding William's childhood had a lasting impact on the boy. The high valley was a perfect nursery for the future translator, and it spoke to him day and night about the glory of its Creator. Looking at his translation of the Bible, it is evident that the poetic clarity of the passages owes something to the plethora of life he witnessed and experienced as a youngster. C. H. Dodd even described Morgan as 'a Hebrew poet of genius.' This is hardly surprising when we think of how some of the psalms of David were influenced by the shepherd boy's own pastoral upbringing.

While William was growing up in the quiet, peaceful valley, Europe was undergoing one of the most turbulent centuries it had yet experienced. There were ruptures in the very establishment and institutions which seemed to hold the old continent together. The Roman Catholic Church was under attack. Erroneous theology and dark practices were being exposed by that force of light which we now call the Protestant Reformation.

Chapter 2:

The Darkest Hour is just before the Dawn

I'm sure that you've heard this familiar proverb before. It's a good description of the spiritual state of Britain before the Reformation. In the next two chapters, we will be looking at this spiritual source of light in some detail. Without the Reformation, William would never have started his translation.

Imagine a grand locomotive – one of those old-fashioned steam trains – something like the Mallard or the Flying Scotsman, a feat of engineering and a powerful unstoppable force. The Reformation was such a machine. So many parts went into its making: cogs, wheels, screws, and pistons. Various components were added over time and, when the machine was ready, the fires were lit. Fuel was shovelled in and wheels started turning. It was an impressive machine, but if there had been no fire in its belly, it would not have gone anywhere.

The fire that the reforming drivers depended on could only come from the Holy Spirit. They were like Elijah who, rather than trusting in numbers and human strength, prayed for heavenly fire on the slopes of Mount Carmel. Why did he do it? '[So] that this people may know that you are the LORD God, and that you have turned their hearts back to you again' (1 Kings 18:37). To continue the metaphor, the drivers were not making their own fires in the locomotive, they were depending on God.

While God is always with us (Deuteronomy 31:6; Matthew 28:20; 1 Corinthians 3:16), there are times in our history when his presence is felt throughout the country. It is supernatural and powerful (Acts 1:8). Once that fire diminishes, the juggernaut keeps on rolling for a while, but its momentum is never the same once its drivers depart from a total reliance on God.

The Dark Age

For more than a thousand years before the Reformation, the Roman Catholic Church and its leaders, called popes, controlled much of Western Europe politically and spiritually. 'The pope was held to be Christ's "vicar" (representative) on earth, and as such, he was the channel through whom all of God's grace flowed.' The prominence of this 'holy father' meant that he ruled like a prince. The clergy held the spiritual power of grace through their seven sacraments. Because of this, they controlled the day-to-day lives of Europe's society. Anyone who resisted ran the risk of losing employment, property, or even their lives.

To put it bluntly, the Roman Catholic Church had departed from scriptural Christianity. Strange doctrines and practices had arisen. Purgatory – a kind of half-way house to heaven – was now an alternative destination after death. Furthermore, the church had even started worshipping saints alongside the Lord Jesus. The cult of the Virgin Mary was the pinnacle of this unbiblical approach. Other things like praying for the dead, the practice of penance, which involves going to a priest and confessing your sins, and making the sign of the cross seeped in over a period of 1600 years. These unbiblical practices enveloped Christian theology and formed, what is commonly called, the 'tradition of the church', which was an alternative source of doctrine that ran parallel to Scripture.

In the context of this book, the saddest result of Roman Catholicism was that the Word of God, the very Scripture which had been graciously given by God as a map guiding us to redemption and heaven, had been taken away from the people. Since the end of the 300s, Latin had become the language of the Western church. The Latin Bible, the *Vulgate* (from *vulgar* meaning 'common' or 'popular') version, was completed in AD 405 by Jerome. The problem was that as the centuries rolled on, fewer and fewer people could speak or read Latin. Only a tiny majority had access to God's Word. The result of this was that the uneducated millions sought their spiritual sustenance from men rather than from God. There truly was, as Amos puts it in chapter 8 verse 11 of his prophecy, a 'famine ... of hearing the words of the LORD'.

A 'Morning Star' – Wycliffe

Perhaps the lasting image of the Reformation is that vivid portrayal of Martin Luther (1483-1546) nailing his ninety five theses to the door of the Wittenberg church. Many often view this event as the great overture to the Reformation. Luther is seen as 'God's Volcano', a man who led the way of reform in the sixteenth century. However, before the likes of Luther, Calvin and Zwingli, we should be made aware of others who were either unhappy with the state of the church or were employed by God as providential cogs contributing to the final locomotive.

One of the greatest of these was a Yorkshireman and theologian called John Wycliffe (c.1330-84), the 'morning star of the Reformation'. We might imagine him in one of the libraries of Oxford University vigilantly penning an important book called *On the Truth of Holy Scripture* (1378). In it he argued that the Bible was the only source of Christian doctrine by which believers should test all the teachings of the church. It seems obvious to us now but, by Wycliffe's time, the Bible had turned into a book for the clergy rather than the people's book. Only priests and theologians could access and interpret its pages. The historian Nick Needham reminds us that 'the Catholic Church looked with great suspicion, even outright hostility, on the idea that a layperson should study the Bible for himself.' The Council of Toulouse (1229) forbad the laity (ordinary people like you and me) from reading the Bible in any language. Translating the Bible was made illegal. Reading, according to the Roman Church, involved having the power to think for yourself and that was far too dangerous.

Wycliffe disagreed. He would argue: 'How can I test the Church if I don't have access to the Bible?' He advocated a return to the original sources not for the glory of culture but for God's glory and for the enlightenment of his compatriots. It was essential for the Latin scriptures to be translated into the native languages of the various nations (the vernacular). Eventually, he organised a team of his disciples to translate the Latin Vulgate Bible into English, a task not finished until after his death. The Wycliffe Bible was a complete translation of the Latin Vulgate into English (1382-95). Every copy

23

was produced by hand. Notice how early these dates are, the 1300s, almost two hundred years before that Reformation locomotive started rolling!

This was revolutionary. No wonder the church hated him so much! By the 1380s, he had bravely rejected the papacy and had even written a pamphlet against transubstantiation – the belief that the bread and wine of the communion service miraculously turns into the real body and blood of our Lord.

For his theology and for his publications, Wycliffe was forced out of his post at Oxford University and he died in 1384. In 1428, the church authorities dug up his body, burnt it on account of his

Portrait of John Wycliffe

'heretical' views, and then threw the ashes into the river Swift. His followers were called 'Wycliffites' or 'Lollards' (a term of abuse which probably meant 'mumblers').

Wycliffe's life has captured the imagination of poets and artists. In 1821, William Wordsworth wrote a sonnet called 'Wicliffe' which focuses on his ashes:

> *As thou these ashes, little Brook! wilt bear*
> *Into the Avon, Avon to the tide*
> *Of Severn, Severn to the narrow seas,*
> *Into main Ocean they, this deed accurst*
> *An emblem yields to friends and enemies*
> *How the bold Teacher's Doctrine, sanctified*
> *By truth, shall spread throughout the world dispersed.*

And the truth did spread. If ever there was a symbol of the 'remnant' in a dark age, Wycliffe would fit the bill.

What about Wales?

Imagine walking into the church in your village or town on a Sunday morning. Your family is by your side as you enter the building with other people gathering from the locality. The minister walks in. The service begins. But there is something very different from what you are used to. In some parts of the service, the language being used is completely unfamiliar to you! It's like watching a film in a foreign language without subtitles! That's what the Sunday experience was like for centuries in Wales.

The Medieval Scriptures

The Welsh translators of the sixteenth century did not work in a vacuum, and we must not view the medieval or pre-Reformation age as being altogether bleak. I want to show you how the foundation of Morgan's work was long in the making and was not always perfect.

The first foundation was not even sacred. A remarkable body of medieval prose literature existed in Welsh on such subjects as laws, legends, romances, history, geography and medicine, all written in a style that was elegant and lucid. More importantly, many religious works, mostly translations from Latin, contained Welsh renderings of the terms and phrases peculiar to Christian theological discourse as well as significant passages from Scripture. Following the Lambeth Council of 1281, it was required that the parish priest expound the doctrines of the church 'in the vernacular and without introducing any fanciful subtleties'. He would do this by reading from various 'gospel' passages in Welsh. Thus, Luke 1: 26-38 was the 'gospel' of the Annunciation of the Blessed Virgin Mary; John 1: 1-14 was the 'gospel' for Christmas; Matthew 26:1-28:7, entitled *y groglith* (the lesson of the cross), corresponded to the 'gospel' for 'the Sunday next before Easter'. It is highly unlikely that these gospels were ever used as the actual 'gospels' read in the Church's Liturgy because that was only done in Latin. But the sermons on

25

these occasions had to be in Welsh so that this is when these readings would probably have been used.

To aid the priests in their various duties, several manuals and tracts were also translated from Latin. Two examples of these that have survived are 'Gwassanaeth Meir' ('The Office of Mary', compiled in c.1400 and 'Y Bibyl Ynghymraec' ('The Bible in Welsh', from the late 13th or early 14th century). The problem with all these selected sources is that the people were being robbed of what God had given to all: the complete revelation of Holy Scripture, namely, the sixty-six books of God's Word. Protestant translators could not rely on these medieval translations. Isaac Thomas explains why:

> *Their use gave no indication of the supreme authority of the Scriptures. They were based not on the original Hebrew and Greek but on the Latin of the Vulgate, a version whose text was frequently uncertain, its translations often ambiguous, and its interpretative glosses far removed from the plain meaning of the original texts. Moreover, the adaptation and paraphrase, the expansion and abridgement which marked these translations diminished the Word of God.*

Chapter 3: After Darkness, Light

T he Renaissance, which means 'revival' or 'rebirth', is the term used to describe the revival of art and learning in the late Middle Ages. Beginning in Italy in the fourteenth century, it had spread throughout Europe by the early sixteenth century. Italian scholars turned to the antiquity of Greece and Rome for their inspiration. Their study of the Early Greek Fathers of the Christian Church eventually brought them back to the Greek texts of the New Testament. In this way, they undermined the authority of the Roman Catholic Church which used the Latin 'Vulgate' translation of the Bible. Because of their more secular approach, with an emphasis on the development of human culture, such scholars were called 'humanists'. But a

true spiritual revival and rebirth did not arise until the coming of the Reformation. People came back to the Lord from a state of darkness and listened to what the Light of the World had to say through his Word. There was a change for the better as a result of this transforming light. Indeed, the very slogan of the Reformation came to be *post tenebras lux*, which means 'after darkness, light'.

The first flicker before the blaze came in the form of the most famous humanist of them all: Erasmus of Rotterdam (1466-1536). In 1516, he went 'back to the sources' and sought to correct the

Desiderius Erasmus

erroneous Latin 'Vulgate'. This resulted in the publication of the Greek New Testament with his own Latin translation alongside. This Greek text would be the precursor to many of our modern translations of the New Testament. The humanist enterprise coincided with the first printing press developed by Johannes Gutenberg around 1450. Quite aptly, the first book to be printed was Gutenberg's Latin Bible. In a way, Erasmus was one of the bridging figures between the Renaissance and the Reformation. Things were moving.

One of the First Drivers – Martin Luther (1483-1546)

Before William Morgan's birth, the Reformation or the true 'Renaissance' would be led by this converted German monk. In a sense, Luther's history is the very story of early Protestantism itself. A grievance and reaction against the erroneous church, mixed with a supernatural conversion, led to a glorious return to biblical Christianity. Let's look at the two events that changed this pious Catholic monk into the great reformer and translator.

The Drum, the Hammer, and the Nail

First, there was the drum! It all started with Luther's disagreement over the selling of indulgences. An indulgence was a way of reducing the amount of punishment people would suffer for their sins in purgatory, that fictitious, non-biblical half-way house between heaven and hell. The Roman Church employed men to travel through Europe to play on people's emotions in order to extract money from them. This great hoax was cloaked in religious language, namely, that loved ones could be released from purgatory if indulgences were bought on their behalf. The indulgence seller travelling around the German lands was a monk called Tetzel who would gather crowds with his drum, and announce loudly: 'When the coin in the coffer rings, the soul from purgatory springs!' Luther was furious with this indulgence market, declaring: 'I want to make a hole in Tetzel's drum!' He realized that if there was any truth in this practice it meant that nobody really needed to repent of their sins.

Then came the hammer and the nail. On All Saints Day 1517, indulgences were to be offered in a town near Wittenberg, where Luther lived as a monk. Luther decided to nail a list of ninety-five theses or arguments, debating the nature of indulgences, on the church door. Whilst not overtly controversial, for Luther was just being a good Catholic at this point, the hammering of these theses on the door would begin a chain-reaction that would eventually lead to Luther rediscovering the doctrine of justification by faith alone.

The Tower Experience

Luther's own journey towards conversion was dogged by his anxiety with regard to 'being right with God'. God was this angry judge who wielded a fiery righteousness which would eventually punish him for his sin. However, something changed. He realized the key role that faith has in salvation. He described his experience, in 1519, when studying Romans 5:17 in a tower room in his monastery:

> *I felt that I was a sinner before God with an extremely disturbed conscience. I could not believe that he was placated by my satisfaction. I did not love, yes, I hated the righteous God who punishes sinners, and secretly, if not blasphemously, certainly murmuring greatly, I was angry with God … Thus I raged with a fierce and troubled conscience. Nevertheless, I beat importunately upon Paul at that place, most ardently desiring to know what St. Paul wanted.*
>
> *At last by the mercy of God, meditating day and night, I gave heed to the context of the words, namely, 'In it the righteousness of God is revealed, as it is written, "He who through faith is righteous shall live."' There I began to understand that the righteousness of God is that by which the righteous lives by a gift of God, namely by faith. And this is the meaning: the righteousness of God is revealed by the gospel, namely, the passive righteousness with which the merciful God justifies us by faith, as it is written, 'He who through faith is*

righteous shall live.' Here I felt that I was altogether born again and had entered paradise itself through open gates.

Michael Reeves comments: 'It was this good news that reformed Luther's heart ... it soon became clear that this discovery not only gave him joy and a quite remarkable confidence; it gave him what can only be seen as a quite superhuman burst of energy to make all this known.'

Luther wrote, wrote and wrote, and he was now writing in German! These truths had to be proclaimed in a language that everyone understood. Between December 1521 and March 1522, whilst he was hiding from his enemies in the Wartburg Castle, Luther managed to complete the first draft of his translation of the New Testament into German. It was published in September 1522.

If Wycliffe and Erasmus were pieces of the locomotive, then Luther was its first driver. He threw coal into the furnace as he went. By letting the Word of God loose among the people, it acted as a combustible fuel, ignited by the Holy Spirit. So began the practice of translating the Bible into the common languages of the world.

Following the publication of the New Testament in German in 1522 and the whole Bible in 1534, a complete translation of the Bible appeared in France in 1530, in the Low Countries in 1527, in England by 1535 thanks to William Tyndale and Miles Coverdale. Then came translations in Danish, Swedish, Finnish, Icelandic, Hungarian, Spanish, Polish, Slovenian, Romanian, Lithuanian and Czech, all by 1593. The locomotive was rolling!

But what about Wales?

As we saw in the second chapter, the Renaissance meant that scholars were returning to the original sources. In 1488, the Hebrew text of the Old Testament had been printed in Northern Italy. In 1516, Erasmus had provided Europe with the Greek New Testament. The tools were there, Wales just needed translators.

William Salesbury and Richard Davies

The first thing God did was to work in the hearts of gifted humanists. The forerunner in the field of Welsh translators came from the same area in North Wales as Morgan, and like him was a great linguist. His name was William Salesbury (c.1520-84).

Born at Cae-Du in the parish of Llansannan, Salesbury hailed from the ranks of the lower gentry. We do not know much about his early years, but he attended Oxford University. A contemporary wrote of him:

> WS I declare is the most learned Briton not only in the British tongue, but in Hebrew, Greek, Latin, English, French, German, and other languages, so much so, that it would be strange that anyone could attain such perfection in the tongues unless he studied nothing else all his life.

According to Eryn White, 'he combined his Protestant humanism with a pride in the Welsh language and concern for its preservation as a language of learning'. It was not just pride but a yearning for spiritual illumination amongst the Welsh, and a realization that he himself had to do something about it.

In 1551, Salesbury published *Kynniver Llith a Ban or Yscrythur Lan* (*As many lessons and articles from the Holy Scripture*). This volume contained Welsh versions of the selection of the Epistles and Gospels contained in the 1549 *Book of Common Prayer*. In the preface, Salesbury bemoans the fact that the Welsh people had so long been deprived of God's Word. So much more needed to be done.

But he couldn't do it alone. Step forward fellow humanist and scholar, Richard Davies (c.1501-81), Bishop of St David's. It is likely that Salesbury and Davies had met at Oxford. Historians call Davies 'the vital catalyst', because he used his position to muster recruits and begin a campaign for the complete translation. A petition (a kind of appeal) to the bishops from before 1563 shows how several committed reformers existed in Wales, all in favour of translating the Scriptures. They argued: *'For the expulsment of sooch*

31

miserable darknes for the lack of the shynyng lyght of Christes Gospell as yet styll remayneth emong the inabitantes of the same Principalite.'

They were driven by that burden for souls – a burden which turned into productivity for the Kingdom of God. A breakthrough came with the act of 1563 for the translation of the Bible into Welsh, which Davies argued for in the House of Lords. We should remember that Queen Elizabeth was interested in its passing in order to guarantee uniformity of religion throughout her realm, especially with the ever-present threat of war breaking out with the Catholic states. Davies argued that Wales could not be easily converted to the Protestant faith without the employment of the only language most of the population could understand. He was a cunning politician, changing his arguments according to his audience at any one time.

Memorial to the translators in St Asaph's Cathedral
Richard Davies (left), William Morgan (right)

1567: The First Breakthrough

What were the outcomes of the bill? The Bible was meant to be published by St David's Day 1567. There was a proviso added which required that every parish church should obtain a copy to be placed alongside the English version, so that parishioners could read and compare. This would have been difficult because most people were illiterate! But at least public worship could now be conducted in Welsh.

In the event, Welsh versions of the New Testament and the *Book of Common Prayer* were ready by 1567, but not the complete Bible. The *Prayer Book* and most of the New Testament was chiefly the work of Salesbury. Davies was responsible for *1 Timothy, Hebrews, James* and *1 and 2 Peter* whilst Thomas Huet, precentor of St David's, worked on the *Book of Revelation*. Their initials appear at the beginning of their contributions. Salesbury writes in the dedication of the New Testament to the Queen that he 'would to God that your Grace's subjects of Wales might also have the whole book of God's word brought to like pass'. Richard Davies declared with some confidence: 'Here is the one part ready, that which is called the New Testament, while you wait, (through God's help that should not be long), the other part, which is called the Old Testament'.

Unfortunately, the 1567 New Testament was unpopular amongst the Welsh. In his desire to display the classical roots of the Welsh language, Salesbury failed to translate the Word into a language that everyone understood. Morris Kyffin wrote that 'the ear of a true Welshman could not bear to hear it'. The whole work was awkward and stilted because Salesbury often ignored linguistic mutation which is used orally to soften the language. His use of archaic language also meant that the common man would have struggled to understand some passages. According to Eryn White:

> It was this reluctance to adopt a more phonetic approach to the written language which marred Salesbury's work and may have been the root cause of his rift with Richard Davies ... [However] Salesbury established many of the principles that would be followed

by subsequent translators who adhered to his policy that, although translators might use modern translations into other languages … they had above all else to remain true to the original.

There was still so much to be done.

Chapter 4:

Two New Environments for William

I t is often tempting to think of William Morgan as a kind of second Samuel who was brought up with the knowledge of the great task that was before him. But what was the spiritual environment existing in the Morgan household? Did Lowri bring William up in the nurture and admonition of the Lord? The simple answer is we do not know. It is likely that the Christianity of Wybrnant was a mix of the old Catholic religion, superstition, and bits of the new theology called 'Protestantism'. It seems as if he was blessed with spiritual sensitivity and an astute intelligence from a young age. Both qualities would be nurtured by God in the coming years. As we've already seen, it was an extremely turbulent time and it must have been quite confusing for everybody living through it.

Some old stories mention William's early spirituality. Near Tŷ Mawr is an outcrop called *Meini Cred* which means the 'rock or stone of belief'. The locals would make the sign of the cross on its surface when passing. According to William's mother, he would often go there while shepherding his father's flocks on Bwlch-y-Groes and she is reported to have said, 'I expect great things of William; I have never seen anyone so careful in their utterance of the Paternoster at *Meini Cred*.' This episode (whether it is true or not) portrays William as a sensitive lad who took spiritual things seriously even when he adhered to the old, superstitious faith.

Lowri was sure that her son would progress once he left Wybrnant. When he was about ten years old, he departed for Gwydir Castle.

Gwydir Castle

The Wynns of Gwydir were an old aristocratic family that had first risen to prominence during the fourteenth century. Their name is often associated with Gwydir Castle, the place William would have most probably called home from 1555 onwards. The most famous member of that family was Sir John Wynn (1553-1627). His dates indicate that he would have grown up alongside William, being eight years younger than him. According to Glanmor Williams, the 'Wynn family kept a school at Gwydir, which seems to have provided an educational springboard for the youthful William Morgan'. In William's youth, the squires would have been John Wyn ap Maredudd (died 1559) and then his son Morus/Maurice (died 1580), who inherited the estate on the death of his father.

The squires kept a chaplain to teach both their own children and the few tenants' sons who showed exceptional promise. I like to think that it was also a kind of thank you to John and Lowri for all their service and hard work that their son was given this educational opportunity. The chaplain, who may have been an old monk, would certainly have taught William the basics of Latin and English, reading, writing, rhetoric, and logic. Some suggest that his future friend, Edmund Prys, might also have received an education at Gwydir Castle around the same time as William. Edmund would later play an important part in Welsh religious history for it was he who produced the *Salmau Gân*, a metrical version of the Psalms in Welsh. This education would have provided them both with a linguistic grounding. Even though Latin was the language that kept so many in the dark, it was also the source of light for scholars. Once the language was learnt, a whole new world of books would be available to the young students.

SIR IOHN WYNNE BARONET.

Sir John Wynn (engraving c.1781)

William and Edmund must have been extremely excited when the opportunity came for both of them to leave for Cambridge. Imagine them packing their things. Many of us have gone through the same process. Whilst we pack our parents' car with all our important possessions, William may have used a mule or a horse. Traditionally, he is meant to have walked the whole way. In a car, and using motorways, the two hundred and fifty miles would probably take something over four hours. To walk would have taken about a week and a half.

Cambridge: The Crucible of Translations

1565 was an eventful year for the Morgan family. William would be leaving Gwydir Castle to study at the prestigious St. John's College, Cambridge. Meanwhile, at home, a building project had begun. The old *tŷ hir Cymreig* of 1520 was being refurbished into a two-storey house. It was beginning to look like the building we see today. The fireplace beam which dominates the main hall was carefully lifted into place whilst an additional floor was added. The house would then have had its fireplaces in the end walls rather than in the middle, as was usually the case in the border counties. It must have improved the family's comfort greatly, being more spacious and warmer. It would also have been healthier with the addition of two chimneys. People had begun to realize the damage a smoky atmosphere did to their lungs. Three mortised collar-beam trusses carrying purlins replaced the lower cruck roof. We don't know how often William came home after his departure from Cambridge but it is likely that he would have seen the home improvements at some point.

Cambridge University was renowned as a centre of scholarship, particularly in the realm of linguistics and theological studies. St. John's had an 'outstanding reputation for the study of Latin, Greek, and Hebrew'. God is good. He led his servant to the best place possible at that time. Some historians believe that he went to London before he commenced his studies at Cambridge. J. Gwilym Jones believed that he may have attended Westminster School in 1564. This was the period that Dr Gabriel Goodman, canon of St Paul's, Dean of Westminster and a scholar and educationalist, was responsible for the students attending that school. There is no evidence for this except for a record denoting that a certain 'Morgan *Maior*' was a student there during Christmas 1564.

It is possible that William and Edmund Prys travelled to Cambridge together for they certainly both registered at St John's early in 1565. According to university registers, William became a *sub-sizar* on the 26 February 1565, and on the 9 June 1565 he was invited to become a *proper sizar*. A *sizar* was originally an undergraduate student who financed his studies by undertaking menial tasks within his college but who later would receive grants from the college. Colleges like St. John's had two categories of *sizar*: a specific number of '*proper sizars*', for whom there were endowments, and *sub-sizars* who were not endowed but maintained by fellow-commoners and fellows.

Fierce Debates

In the 1560s, the university was rife with fierce debates between the Puritans, the faction within the Church of England who wished to see further reform, especially in the areas of priestly vestments and church government, and the 'official' party which supported the Elizabethan Religious Settlement of 1559. St. John's College was one of the bastions of Puritanism. On one Sunday in December 1565, for instance, some of the students and fellows came into the college chapel not wearing their surplices. Geraint Gruffydd notes that William 'refused to discard his surplice during the puritan demonstrations'.

The Puritan leader in Cambridge at that time was Thomas Cartwright (1535-1603), while the more traditional, Anglican leader was John Whitgift (1530-1604). We know that William would become very close to Whitgift, the future Archbishop of Canterbury. Indeed, in God's providence, Whitgift would be instrumental in the translation process. By 1570, Whitgift's party was victorious and they stripped Cartwright of his chair after he had openly called for Presbyterianism in the Church of England. We should remember that both gentlemen were ardent Protestants but with differing views on church government and rituals. It is difficult for us, today, to esteem Whitgift highly, especially knowing that it was his signature that appeared on the death warrant of John Penry (1559-93), Wales' most famous Protestant martyr.

Studies and Teachers

What kind of subjects did William study? For his BA, he would have concentrated on mathematics before moving on to rhetoric and logic in his second year. In his third and final year, he focused on philosophy. He then continued to study for his master's degree which would see the young man shifting towards Greek, Hebrew, further philosophy and astronomy. It was at Cambridge that his study of languages intensified. Some scholars suggest that eventually he may have spoken at least nine languages including Welsh, English, Hebrew, Greek, Aramaic, French, German, and Italian. Perhaps the most important language that Morgan mastered was Hebrew, the language of most of the Old Testament. There is some debate as to who actually would have taught him this ancient tongue.

There is a tradition that the leading European Hebraist scholar and Calvinist, John Immanuel Tremellius (c.1510-80) and onetime professor of Hebrew at Cambridge, taught William for a short time when he returned to England around 1565-66 due to a plague in the university of Heidelberg where he worked. Following his conversion to Christianity from Judaism, Tremellius rose to prominence in the mid-sixteenth century as a professor of Hebrew and Old Testament studies. He was one of Europe's most celebrated men because of his work in translating the Syriac New Testament and the Hebrew Old Testament into Latin.

William's main tutor, however, was probably the Huguenot and former assistant to Tremellius, Antoine Rodolph Chevallier (1523-72) who was appointed reader in Hebrew at Cambridge in 1569. 'Huguenot' is the name given to Calvinistic French Protestants of the sixteenth and seventeenth centuries. Many of them had to flee their homeland because of Catholic persecution. Eventually many of the Huguenots settled in Protestant countries like the Netherlands and Great Britain. After studying in Paris under the humanist François Vatable, Chevallier came to Britain and settled in Cambridge during the reign of Edward VI. According to the theologian, Hugh Broughton, who had been his pupil: 'men might learn more of him in a month than others could teach in ten years.'

In William's time, the university provided the graduate with a full and rich education. There would have been a combination of classical studies together with the theological studies which we would expect for a theological student. The idea of just studying one subject was simply not good enough! By 1583, William had achieved four degrees from the University of Cambridge: B.A., M.A., B.D. and D.D.

Key Contacts

Richard Vaughan,
Bishop of Bangor

John Whitgift,
Archbishop of Canterbury

In the book of Proverbs, we are told that 'He who walks with wise men will be wise, but the companion of fools will be destroyed' (Proverbs 13:20). In Cambridge, William identified himself with the group of young men who shared his interest in spiritual things. They also had other mutual interests such as languages, translation, theology and Wales! In God's providence, these friends and acquaintances would help William with the future translation.

Indeed, if the Wybrnant was the 'translator's nursery', then Cambridge became the 'translation's crucible.' Among his contemporaries at St. John's were two gifted North Walians: Richard Vaughan (1550-1607) and, as we have seen, Edmund Prys (c.1542-1623). Vaughan would later become bishop of Bangor, then Chester, and finally, London. Prys became the archdeacon of Meirioneth and translated the Psalms into Welsh metrical verse. It is pleasant to speculate that Morgan and Prys might have started translating the Psalms together while studying Hebrew at St. John's. It seems like a good place to begin. I can almost imagine the two lads debating the ancient words in the candlelight.

At Cambridge, Morgan also met Gabriel Goodman (1528-1601), Dean of Westminster since 1561; William Hughes (d.1600), Bishop of St Asaph from 1573; and Hugh Bellot (1542-96), Bishop of Bangor between 1585-95. Perhaps the most important meeting of all was William's introduction to John Whitgift, the so-called 'ruler of Cambridge', who served as Master of Trinity College in the 1570s, but as Archbishop of Canterbury from 1583 to 1604. All these men would give much assistance in the venture that Morgan was soon to begin.

William was probably persuaded of the doctrines of God's grace in the salvation of sinners while at Cambridge. This might have come about during his long conversations with Chevallier, or perhaps through his introduction to the teaching of Calvin and Luther which he found in the books and pamphlets which were available to him there. No testimony of his spiritual experience has survived. What is certain is that by the time of his ordination in 1568 he believed in *Evangelium Christi* – the Gospel of our Lord and Saviour Jesus Christ.

"Canmolwn yn awr y gwŷr enwog"
WILLIAM MORGAN 1541-1604 Bishop of St.Asaph, who translated the Bible from the original languages into Welsh.
EDMWND PRYS 1541-1623, Archdeacon of Meirioneth, who translated the Hebrew Psalms into Welsh verse.
Members of this College, lifelong friends, and fellow-workers in a great task
"Disgwyliaf o'r mynyddoedd draw Lle daw im help 'wyllysgar"

Plaque in St John's College, Cambridge

Chapter 5: Homeward Bound

On concluding his studies at Cambridge, William was about twenty-three years of age. It would seem appropriate to refer to him as Morgan from now on. Unlike many of his peers, he seems to have acquired a specific burden for his own country. Personally, I think he came back to Wales with the sole intent of preparing for the translation. It seems logical to be working on a Welsh-language translation in the place where Welsh would have been spoken daily. Whilst some historians believe that his motives for translating were driven by politics, I firmly believe that he had a deep yearning for the spiritual well-being of his people. God drew him home and he returned to a land that desperately needed his skills and energy.

Morgan started ministering in the Church of England before finishing his studies at Cambridge. He was ordained at Ely Cathedral around 1568. The declaration he made at Ely when he was ordained would be the driving force behind his whole career as a preacher and Bible translator. According to the historians: 'he expressed his wish to be a deacon out of "zeal to God his word" [or, in modern English, "zeal to God's word"] and proclaimed his faith that 'Evangelium Christi est potentia Dei ad salutem omni credenti' ('The gospel of Christ is the power of God unto everyone that believeth', Romans 1:16). It is interesting to note that William Salesbury had included the same text on the title page of his *Kynniver Llith a Ban* in 1551. It is very possible that Morgan already saw himself as an heir to the earlier Welsh translators. He had now picked up the baton and begun the work where Salesbury and Davies had left off. It is heart-warming to see these little 'fish marks' on the pages of history. I cannot believe that the repetition of Romans 1:16 is just some form of etiquette. I think it must have been Morgan's 'calling verse' as it were, because, once again, it was given pride of place on the title-page of his New Testament in 1588. Just like our brothers and sisters in the first century Roman catacombs, Morgan is saying: 'I am a Christian. I believe in the gospel of our Lord Jesus Christ.'

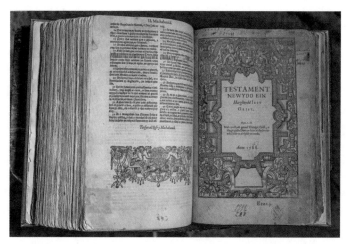

Title page of the *New Testament* in the 1588 Welsh Bible

When he came home to Wales, Morgan did not return to the refurbished Tŷ Mawr, Wybrnant. The first church that he was associated with was Llanbadarn Fawr in the diocese of St David's. He was *collated* at the age of twenty-seven on 29 December 1572. This means that he was given a living by the Church of England for some services rendered. At that time, the bishop of St David's, the man who would have appointed him to the post, was none other than Richard Davies, whom we have met previously. It is possible that Davies was looking for young talented men who would be able to help him in translating the Old Testament.

In 1575, the year that Salesbury and Davies quarrelled over their translation, Morgan moved to the diocese of St Asaph and became the vicar of Welshpool. Bishop William Hughes, a contemporary of Morgan, was looking for gifted preachers and most historians agree that Morgan was powerfully used in the pulpit. According to the historian, Glanmor Williams, 'Morgan throughout his life proved to be a preacher of exceptional prowess'. The poet Huw Machno wrote:

I bregethu, brig ieithoedd,
Ugain llu, y gannwyll oedd.

He was the pinnacle of languages
In preaching to many, he was the candle.

The poet uses 'Reformation' language here. North Wales was spiritually dark in the sixteenth century and, while recognizing Morgan's earthly gifts, he is, more importantly, emphasizing the light of the gospel. The man who left for Cambridge had returned as a young preacher.

A decade after his ordination, Morgan finally assumed the responsibilities of a full-time parish priest when he took up residence at the vicarage which has become synonymous with his name: Llanrhaeadr-ym-Mochnant, in the old county of Denbighshire, which he held with neighbouring Llanarmon Mynydd Mawr. The name Llanrhaeadr-ym-Mochnant means the 'church of the waterfall in the stream of pigs' – quite a vivid place-name! Morgan would spend the next sixteen years in this parish, translating the Bible and serving the community as pastor. It was a long way from any university, library or centre of cultural and economic activity but it would prove an important centre for the work that was at hand.

Marriage

One strange tradition of the past had it that Morgan was a bachelor throughout his whole life! This is a myth. We know for certain that he married a lady called Catherine, the daughter of George ap Richard ap John from Oswestry. According to some historians of the past, this was his second wife. Reference is made to an Ellen Salesbury, daughter to Dafydd Salesbury of Llanberis, whom he is supposed to have married in secret before leaving for Cambridge. This theory, put forward by an early biographer, Charles Ashton, in 1891, is fascinating in that it would link our two translators, Salesbury and Morgan, by marriage! If Ashton is correct, Ellen was William Salesbury's niece. However, if he did marry Ellen, she must have died quite early on because we know he was married to Catherine by the time he took up his position at Llanrhaeadr. Earlier scholars believed that a certain Evan was the issue of that first marriage. However, most historians now believe that

Evan Morgan was in fact the son of William's eldest brother. Evan became vicar of Llanrhaeadr in March 1597, canon of Llandaff by 1598 and precentor by 1600. It is unlikely that William had any children of his own. Catherine was a good helpmeet to William throughout his career as parish minister and then as bishop. The poets sang of their warm hospitality and they were famed for their generosity.

A Bitter Argument

Unfortunately, as for many pastors, Morgan's time at Llanrhaeadr was burdened by social tensions. A bitter feud ensued between him and one of the local noblemen, so much so that Morgan for a time felt that he had to carry a pistol under his cassock in church! It started when Morgan became a witness in a case of adultery or an unlawful marriage against a certain Ifan Maredudd of Llansilin. The case was first brought to the attention of Bishop William Hughes before reaching Whitgift who was, at the time, Bishop of Worcester and vice-president of the Council in the Marches at Ludlow. It didn't help that Morgan had arranged a marriage between one of the sons of Sir John Wynn of Gwydir and Catrin, daughter of Dafydd Llwyd, a wealthy local heiress whom Ifan Maredudd's nephew was intending to marry.

Things got worse. During the 1590s, Morgan took Maredudd to the Star Chamber, which was an important English court that sat at Westminster, accusing him of malice, abusing his position as an attorney, interfering with some footmen that Morgan was meant to be training, and even attacking Morgan's curate, Lewis Hughes, in the middle of the night. Ifan Maredudd's response to the last accusation was that he had simply called on Hughes that night to ask him whether he could use his harp for an evening of merry-making, a *noson lawen* as the Welsh call it, in the local tavern! Maredudd then presented a counter-case against Morgan accusing him of a long list of misdemeanours including making money at the expense of his parishioners, keeping riotous servants and beating his mother-in-law. He refers to Catherine, Morgan's wife as:

A wafer woman [who] went up and down from town to town, from alehouse to alehouse, and from wine tavern to wine tavern with a basket under her arm selling wafers ... [She is] a woman of the lightest conversation, lewdest order of life, loosest behaviour of any woman that in the memory of man ever dwelt in the country where she now dwelleth.

Morgan rejected these malicious accusations, but he did admit to giving his mother-in-law 'a little flick or pat upon the chin' when she rebuked his servants for not attacking Maredudd's men! This must have been a difficult period for Morgan.

He was also accused of being uncharitable. Maredudd claimed that he would put on a great show of giving bread and broth to the poor on Sunday, but would then, 'with a great mastiff', send away everyone who came to his door during the week! These accusations are amusing to us and they seem unlikely especially when the poets, Siôn Tudur, Owain Gwynedd, Ifan Tew and Siôn Mawddwy, unanimously praised Morgan and his wife for their great generosity. The truth would seem to be that Maredudd never forgave Morgan for being a witness in the earlier case. Ultimately, Sir John Wynn managed to reconcile the two parties, but the quarrel had taken a considerable toll on Morgan in more ways than one. Thankfully, the episode did not interfere with the important work that he had begun.

Chapter 6: Translating the Bible

There has been considerable debate with regard to the year Morgan started his great work. Many scholars believe that it was unlikely to have been before 1578 because only by then would he have acquired the necessary skills for the mammoth task. However, they forget that mastering a language like Hebrew involves the exercising of translation skills from the very outset. Whilst there is no concrete evidence, it seems probable that Morgan may have prepared, or even begun, some elements of the translation while at Cambridge.

Why then was there the long delay between his return to Wales in 1572 and the publication of the Bible in 1588? Morgan gives numerous clues with respect to the reasons for the delay in his dedication to Elizabeth I printed in the 1588 translation. Firstly, he writes that he had been persuaded to undertake the task only when it became apparent that no other translation would follow on from the 1567 New Testament. He also mentions other factors:

> *When therefore I saw that the translation of the rest of the Scriptures was so useful, nay so necessary (though long deterred by the sense of my weakness, and the magnitude of the work, as well as the evil disposition of certain people) yielding to the wishes of the pious, I allowed myself to be persuaded to undertake this most important, troublesome and to many, unacceptable task.*

Morgan is quite open about his own 'weakness'. This suggests that he was overwhelmed with the task before him. What needed to be done? The translation of the whole Hebrew Old Testament (except the Psalms), and of all the Greek and Latin books of the Apocrypha into Welsh for the first time, along with a revision of Salesbury's Psalms and 1567 New Testament!

He also mentions the 'evil disposition of certain people'. This may refer to the troubles he encountered with his neighbour, Ifan Maredudd. It may also include the opposition he felt from within the church and from some elements of the government. Some were suspicious of Welsh and other British languages other than English in a period when the idea of one language was of paramount importance for maintaining the Union. The question of language and nationalism is not a recent phenomenon. Morgan answers some of these critics in the dedication:

> *If there are any who maintain that in order to retain agreement our countrymen had better learn the English tongue than that the Scriptures should be translated into our own, I would wish that while they study unity, they would be more cautious not to hinder the truth, and while they are most anxious to promote concord they should not put religion on one side. For although it is much to be desired that the inhabitants of the same island should be of the same speech and tongue, yet it is to be equally considered that to attain this end so much time and trouble are required, that in the meantime God's people would be suffered to perish from hunger of His word which would be barbarous and cruel beyond measure. Further there can be no doubt that similarity and agreement in religion rather than in speech much more promotes unity.*

Sometimes it is suggested that Morgan's priority was the saving of the Welsh language; that he was a conscious pioneer of language conservation. This is not the case. While the Bible did turn out to be the salvation of the Welsh language, Morgan's aim was not the redeeming of a dying tongue but, rather, the avoiding of the kind of famine to which the prophet Amos refers: a famine of God's Word.

An Imaginative Visit

Let's visit his study in the Llanrhaeadr-ym-Mochnant vicarage. This is always my favourite room to visit when in someone's house! Scrolls and papers are scattered everywhere. The paper is thick and expensive. It looks like the vellum that monks used to write on. There's a large quill made from a white goose feather and a glass ink-well on the table. There's also a copy of the seventh volume of the Antwerp Polyglot Bible lying open. This includes the Hebrew text, as well as Pagninus' Latin version adapted to give a word for-word translation. By looking at these texts, Morgan can find the dictionary meaning of every Hebrew word, but a good knowledge of Hebrew vocabulary and syntax is still vital if he's going to arrive at the correct meaning. What else is on his desk? – the Latin versions by Tremellius, Estienne and Münster. These would have been extremely helpful. There's another table to one side – yes, more books! – on which is a precious copy of the Geneva Bible from 1560. This is the same Bible that William Shakespeare, John Donne, Oliver Cromwell and even John Bunyan, later, would have used. In addition, there's a copy of the Bishops' Bible of 1568 as an extra reference.

There's more here. What's this? These are very interesting: copies of Theodore Beza's Bible, together with an earlier Hebrew Bible printed in Venice in 1524-25. Like his English counterpart, William Tyndale, Morgan hunted high and low for any source of information that would help him find the most accurate meaning of the Hebrew and Greek words with which he was dealing.

The Difficulty of the Task

We know that Morgan almost despaired of his task after finishing the first five books of the Bible but Whitgift persuaded him to persevere:

> *But I had scarcely taken it in hand, when overwhelmed by the difficulty of the work and the greatness of the expense, I should have succumbed (as they say) on the very threshold and issued only the Pentateuch from the press but that had it not been that the Most Reverend Father in Christ, the Archbishop of Canterbury, that most-excellent patron of learning [and] most keen champion of the truth.*

Whitgift was proving a useful ally to Morgan and their relationship would continue to be invaluable for the translation. Not only was he by now Archbishop but he also had very close ties with Queen Elizabeth. She nicknamed him her 'little black husband' because of his dark complexion, and the Archbishop of York noted 'her special good affection towards him'. Whitgift also had the authority to establish the Bible's eventual use in the church.

What about the New Testament? We have already mentioned some of the weaknesses in the 1567 version. Morgan needed to revise, correct and refine its language. This was no small task. According to Isaac Thomas:

It [was] guided by the following principles: that a translation of the Scriptures should deviate as little as possible from the exact wording and syntax of the original; that variety in expression and especially in orthography should be limited; that the familiar Welsh usage in vocabulary and syntax is preferable to what is archaic or foreign or strange; that new word-formations are acceptable if needed and their meaning readily understood; that the Welsh literary sentence should follow the abnormal pattern and have a finite verb which should always be in agreement with its subject in person and number; that the standard in orthography should be that of strict-metre poetry but that some shortened oral forms were quite acceptable.

That may sound complicated, but it can be summarised by two words: accuracy and faithfulness. As mentioned, Morgan had access to newer Latin versions published since 1567 as well as Beza's 1582 Greek text and Latin version. Of course, he would have closely consulted the 1567 edition since Salesbury and Davies had done so much of the groundwork. We must also never forget that Morgan's work would always have been accompanied by much prayer. Translation is not just an intellectual exercise. He was handling the very words of God and I am sure that he would have been very aware of the necessary attitude of humility and submission before the Word, in order to handle it rightly.

Was he alone?

Not entirely. In his *Dedication* of the Bible, Morgan acknowledged the help he received from several friends:

The names of those who more especially have endeavoured to promote this work. The Reverend Fathers, the Bishops of St. Asaph and Bangor [his old Cambridge friends, William Hughes and Hugh Bellot, respectively], who have both of them lent me the books for which I asked, and have condescended to examine, weigh and approve of this work. Gabriel Goodman, Dean of Westminster, truly a good man in name and in deed, and most devoted of all in piety, when I was translating, paid such attention when I read it over to him, that he greatly assisted me by his labour and advice, gave me a large number of his own books, and for a whole year while the book was in the press (with the most kindly consent of the College) afforded me hospitality, which kindness the Most Reverend Archbishop [John Whitgift], of whom I made mention before in this epistle, offered me most generously, but I had to refuse on account of the river Thames which keeps apart and separates his house from the printers.

So also no little help was given by these,
David Powel, Doctor of Divinity
Edmund Price, Archdeacon of Merioneth
Richard Vaughan, of St. John's College, which is Rector of Lutterworth.

Most of the names listed here are already familiar to us. You may have spotted his old friend, Edmund Prys. He would have been well-placed to advise Morgan on the original languages and the tricky questions when translating them into Welsh. You will also notice that many of these friends lent books to one another. This wasn't just a friendly gesture but a practical way of keeping costs down and making sure that every scholar had all the information necessary. It was an example of the warmest kind of teamwork amongst like-minded people, driven by a higher calling than mere academic and scholastic interest or ambition.

One of Morgan's talents was his ability to identify such capable young men to assist him in his work. Mention should be given to John Dafis of

Llanferres and Jasper Gryffyth of Guilsfield. These two young men became his amanuenses and were vitally important in assisting him in the work. In that earlier study scene, there would be additional tables where these scholars would have assisted their master. No early modern study would be complete without such learned helpers.

St Dogfan's Church, Llanrhaeadr-ym-Mochnant

Chapter 7: Finishing the Work

The late 1580s had been difficult years for Wales. There was a severe famine in the years 1585-86, and many had interpreted this as a sign of God's wrath. Politically also, things were tense. Some Welshmen had been involved in the Babington Plot of 1586 which led to the execution of Mary Stuart and brought Spain and England to the brink of total war. Elizabeth's kingdom had never felt more fragmented.

Historians believe that by 1587 the Welsh Bible project was not only being encouraged by John Whitgift, but that he was actively seeking to hurry Morgan in his work. He pressed Morgan to stay with him at Lambeth Palace even before the translation was finished! It is evident that he wanted a speedy publication of the Bible. There were three particular reasons why Whitgift was in such a hurry.

A Fragmented Britain

Ironically, by trying to unify Britain, Henry VIII had probably created a significant division. The Laws in Wales Acts of 1535 and 1542 (commonly known as the Acts of Union) were parliamentary measures which resulted in Wales being officially annexed to England. Henry VIII wanted a single state. One consequence of this was that the Welsh language now no longer had official status. This would no doubt have agitated some of the Welsh. Elizabeth inherited this problem and hoped that a Welsh Bible could be a uniting tool or an acceptable peace-offering. Here was the Defender of the New Faith providing her subjects with the Word of God in their tongue. This was a monarch who gave something back to her loyal subjects. But in fact, she had mixed motives: as well as defending the Faith, she was seeking to ensure that her realm would not be fragmented.

The Catholic Threat

Whitgift was conscious also of a possible Catholic resurgence in Wales. We should not forget that Henry VIII had abandoned the Church of Rome in the early 1530s because of the Pope's refusal to annul his marriage to Catherine of Aragon. This action would have been extremely difficult for many of the Welsh to stomach. Here again, Elizabeth inherited her father's predicament. It is possible that Wales could have developed into a Catholic threat. The country was a long way behind England in its attitude to the Reformation. Not only were the majority secretly loyal to the old faith, but, geographically, it took longer for ideas to reach western Britain. It is no accident that Puritan activity during the sixteenth and seventeenth centuries tended to emerge in the border towns or in other centres of commerce. In other places, old ways and habits would have died hard.

Some loyal Catholics sought to counter the Reformation in Wales by using the same techniques that had been most effective for the Protestants on mainland Europe, in particular, printing. One year after Salesbury's Testament of 1567, Morys Clynnog published the Catholic *Athrauaeth Gristnogaul* in Milan. Similarly, one year before William Morgan's *Bible*, the first book to be printed on Welsh soil, *Y Drych Cristianogawl* (*The Christian Mirror*) emerged, in 1587, from a secret printing press hidden in one of the caves of Rhiwledyn rocks near Llandudno. The book was written by a certain G. R., again from Milan. This was either Gruffydd Robert (c.1532-98), or a priest called Robert Gwyn, originally from the Pwllheli area. The three-part book sought to educate the Welsh in the Catholic doctrine with regard to the four last things: death, judgement, heaven and hell. It was a pocket-sized book of only 180 pages.

First page of *Y Drych Cristianogawl* (1587)

Printing this book must have been both daunting and exciting. The cave could only be approached from the sea. All the equipment needed to be transported in small boats. Fortunately, a Catholic nobleman called Robert Pue of Penrhyn Creuddyn owned the land, and it is possible he supported the venture. The name of the printer was Robert Thackwell. Everything was ready for the precious copies to be distributed.

And then – disaster! On 14 April 1587, Good Friday, the authorities discovered the cave. They waited at its mouth all night. For some reason they were afraid of attacking it at night, even with forty men at their disposal. By morning, the Catholic printers had escaped. It would take months before they were eventually apprehended. Unfortunately, this cave has disappeared in the intervening centuries. It was probably destroyed during quarrying activity in the area before the First World War.

But Catholicism and the Acts of Union were not the only reasons why Whitgift hurried Morgan along. There was another revolutionary voice which Whitgift had to silence.

John Penry – A voice crying in the wilderness

According to Glanmor Williams:

> It could conceivably have been Penry's deadly shafts, added to the other perils of the time, which spurred Whitgift to a greater sense of urgency and forced him to realize the desperate need to counter-attack Penry and other Puritans on the one hand, and the Catholics on the other, by publishing a Welsh Bible.

How could one man be such an annoyance for Whitgift? The man in question was a young Puritan preacher called John Penry (c.1563-93). He had been educated in Cambridge and Oxford before eventually becoming a university preacher. When he entered Cambridge, it was claimed that there was never a more 'arrant a Papist as ever came out of Wales', but while at university, Penry had been deeply convicted of sin and of the need of divine grace. He speaks of himself as one of those who 'have known a remission of our sinnes, even of our great sinnes'.

Now a Calvinistic Puritan, Penry had a high view of Scripture: all of it was inspired and was the only guide, not only for doctrine and morals, but also for the forms of church government and religious worship. During his time at Cambridge, he had been struck by the desperate spiritual condition of Wales, realizing, what the Elizabethan government itself conceded in parliamentary reports of 1563 that the people of Wales, 'utterly destituted of Goodes holy woorde, doo remayne in the like, or reyther more Darckness and Ignorance, then they were in the tyme of Papistrye'. What a terrible admission!

In the spring of 1587, Penry submitted a petition to the Queen and Parliament drawing attention to the religious condition of Wales. It was called *A Treatise containing the Aequity of an Humble Supplication* and its main theme was the desperate need for more preachers. Penry was arrested because of Whitgift's opposition to the book and appeared before the Court of High Commission before later being released.

Penry then wrote two further works in the 1580s admonishing the rulers of Wales in plain terms as to what would befall them if they neglected to carry out their duties. He testified how he himself had been 'begotten into the Church of God' through hearing the gospel preached, and that he longed for this blessing to be shared by his countrymen.

Unfortunately, Penry's books were printed by the same press that had produced the *Martin Marprelate tracts*, fifty or more publications which advocated Puritan principles, but attacked the bishops in crude, satirical language. Penry, of course, was suspected of being one of the authors of these tracts. Historians now agree that he could never have written them 'for they made their readers laugh at sin, whereas to Penry sin was odious'. But it was these tracts and his associations with the Separatists, who opposed an exclusive state church in favour of the gathering together of believers to form local churches, that eventually led to his arrest in 1593. He was charged with seeking to overthrow religion and 'fomenting treason and rebellion'. Whitgift signed the warrant of his execution on the 29 May 1593 and, on the same day, he was hanged. He was only thirty years old.

A week before he died, Penry had written:

> *I am a poore young man borne and bredd in the mountaynes of Wales. I am the first since the last springing up of the Gospell in this latter age that publicly laboured to have the blessed seed thereof sowen in these barrayn mountaynes … And now being to end my dayes before I am come unto the one half of my yeeres in the lykely course of nature, I leave the successe of these my labours unto such of my Contreymen, as the Lord is to rayse up after mee for the accomplishing of that worke, wch in the calling of my contrey unto the knowledge of Christs blessed Gospell I beganne.*

God had already answered that prophetic prayer. Morgan not only gave Wales its much-needed translation but would later ensure that preaching returned to the pulpits of his dioceses. Furthermore, God would raise up many more men who would continue to call the people of Wales into the 'knowledge of Christ's blessed Gospel'.

Morgan arrives in London

The 1588 translation is finished. We can imagine what happened then.

The papers are tied with cords and they are placed carefully in large wooden chests. 'Lewis, will you help me with this chest?' William's curate has just arrived to help with the precious load. The papers are thick and they don't all fit in one chest. 'When are they passing by?' asks Morgan, looking again through the window. 'Oh, in the next hour I think, sir. We'll move everything to the crossroads so you can be ready'. 'I don't want to miss them'. He rushes from the window, checking his papers one last time.

Morgan did not send his curate to London with the manuscript, he was waiting for the drovers. Not those travelling from the west, passing the doors of Wybrnant on their way, but drovers from the north, passing through Llanrhaeadr to meet up with the others on the London road. Nor would he entrust the precious papers to them. He would go to London himself. It was crucial that he should be there to supervise the progress of the manuscript through the press. This was the Word of God after all. He would be both proof-corrector and author of the text. Such a dual role was quite rare in the publishing business back then, but in this case it was absolutely necessary. Who, in London, could have undertaken the proof-reading of the Welsh text? Local tradition maintains that Morgan travelled to London in the company of a group of drovers. This makes complete sense. The roads were dangerous, especially if you were a person of some means. Travelling in numbers would have been much safer. It was a long way and the company would have been most welcome. There is no record of his thoughts and experiences on that journey, but perhaps we can imagine the scene.

The road is bumpy. The journey seems to last forever. The bearded scholar sits on the cart and, from the corner of his eye, he checks whether the papers are still safely stowed in the chests. The cattle are making a lot of noise and they sometimes bump against the cart. One of the drovers passes him some food – a piece of cheese with some bread.

As he eats the meal, he thinks about the difference this book will make in his country. He knows that there are problems. He knows that many still follow the old religion. He also knows that many follow no God at all. He remembers his early days and how he used to climb up beyond *Meini Cred* and say his *Paternoster*. He'd never heard about the wealth of Scripture back then; he'd only recited his set prayers like a good boy. It wasn't the same as knowing God. He meditates about the depth of the Old Testament stories and how they point to the Messiah. He sees similarities between Wales and Israel especially in their constant departure from God. He thinks of the time when the Book of the Law had been lost in the days of the wicked kings, Manasseh and Amon, and remembers translating 2 Kings 22:10-11: 'Then Shaphan the scribe showed the king saying, "Hilkiah the priest has given me a book". And Shaphan read it before the king. Now it happened, when the king heard the words of the Book of the Law, that he tore his clothes.'

Would there be a similar reaction when his translation is published at last? Would there be a return to God by the people of Wales? He certainly hopes so. It's still a long way to London and he prays for protection. He has no need now to touch any sacred stones but, sitting in the cart, with the cows walking quietly alongside, he closes his eyes and prays to his Father in heaven.

When he reached London, it's likely that he visited the Archbishop to notify him of the completion of the translation. Whitgift would have been thrilled. We know from the dedication that Whitgift had shouldered a considerable share of the cost involved in printing the volume. Having paid his respects to the Archbishop, Morgan would then have crossed the Thames and knocked on Gabriel Goodman's door in Westminster. His good friend had invited him to stay at his house while the Bible was being printed. The house was conveniently close to the printers. It made sense to stay there. His year with Goodman would have been a happy time of fellowship for them both.

The printer was a certain Christopher Barker, 'printer to the Quennes most excellent maiestie' who then delegated the work to a man called George Bishop. The Bible would be printed at the press at the sign of the Bell in St. Paul's churchyard. The Barkers were the same printing family that oversaw production of the Geneva and Bishops' Bibles during Elizabeth's reign. Latin: a tick. Greek: a tick. English: a tick. Welsh? This would be a bit trickier. The thought of having to print Welsh in those days must have been a nightmare for any Englishman. George Bishop must have been very relieved when Morgan turned up to help.

The printing would be a long process, requiring time management, organization and concentration. It also required several different workers: some to set the letters; some to ink them; some to prepare the paper; some to work the press. Each individual letter was selected to make up the words, the words set into sentences, and all constructed on a tablet. This was then inked with French ink onto paper imported from either Normandy or Champagne. Morgan would have been there, constantly checking the proofs for any mistakes. The papers would be hung to dry and then eventually taken to the binder.

The text was printed in beautiful black lettering with illustrations and various designs at book and chapter headings. The binder would have taken the leaves and bound them in leather on a wooden base. The result was a bulky, folio volume of 1,122 pages, containing the Old and New Testaments and Apocrypha. The edition ran to 1,000 copies which is a considerable print run when you consider the time and effort put into every single page. Each copy was sold at the cost of £1, 'the cost to be jointly borne by the incumbent and the parishioners in the case of parish churches'. The whole process took a year to complete.

It was a good translation. In fact, most agree that it was excellent. Morgan had set out to translate the Hebrew and Greek texts as faithfully and as accurately as he could, but without sacrificing intelligibility in doing so. At last, the Welsh had a Bible written in their own living language.

On the 22 September 1588, the Privy Council issued instructions that letters be dispatched to the four Welsh bishops and the Bishop of Hereford. These letters were to inform them that the 'translation of the Bible into the Welsh or British tongue, which, by the Act of Parliament should long since have been done, is now performed by one Doctor William Morgan and set forth in print'.

Statue of Bishop Morgan in the City Hall, Cardiff

Chapter 8:   The Bishop's Legacy

We have reached the final chapter of Morgan's life but not the final chapter of the translation. It is believed that in 1603, one year before Morgan died, he completed a revision of his New Testament and sent it to be printed in London. Unfortunately, in the disorder which followed the plague of 1603, the manuscript was lost. God's ways are not our ways. It would fall to the great Dr John Davies, Mallwyd, and Bishop Richard Parry to complete the next revision which would come to be known as the 1620 Bible, the version with which we are most familiar, and which most of us continue to attribute to Morgan. This is the version which is held in the same long-standing regard in Wales as the King James Version in England. The stories of Davies and Parry are worth telling, but that is a subject for another day.

Promotion

Following the completion of the translation, Morgan was made a bishop. He was not the perfect bishop, in the biblical sense of being a caring overseer and shepherd over his flock, but, according to the standard of the time, he had a good reputation. The occasion of his promotion was the removal, in 1594, of Gervase Babington, Bishop of Llandaff, to the see of Exeter. There was a need for a replacement in South Wales and Morgan was chosen. It is said that the Queen herself wished Morgan to follow Babington. Sir John Wynn, typically, insinuated that he was the one responsible for securing the bishopric for him: 'his first preferment was with myself and by my means,' he says in his *Memoirs* and, in a letter to Morgan, 'If I had not pointed you the way with my finger … you had been still the Vicar of Llanrhaeadr'. Morgan would stay in Llandaff for the next six years.

William and Catherine resided at Mathern, near Chepstow, and were, according to the poets, as hospitable there as they had previously been in

Llanrhaeadr. On 18 November 1600, William Hughes, Bishop of St Asaph, died. Within the month, Gabriel Goodman, whom we have seen was William's close friend, wrote to Robert Cecil, Elizabeth's Secretary of State, recommending Morgan for the post:

> *My lord of Llandaff is well known to be the most sufficient man in that country both for his learning, government and honesty of life, and hath also best deserved of our country for his great pains and charges in translating the Bible into our vulgar tongue, with such sufficiency as deserveth great commendation and reward.*

And Whitgift wrote:

> *[Morgan is] a man of integrity, gravity and great learning, for whom he has received that testimony, both from the best of that country where he now remains, and of that also where he wishes him to be placed, that he never received for any man.*

He was elected on 21 July 1601 and enthroned on the 21 September. His new position meant that his salary nearly doubled since the appointment included the position of Archdeacon of St Asaph as well as the bishopric.

William and Catherine moved to Plas Gwyn, the Archdeacon's house at Dyserth, in the old county of Flintshire, because the episcopal palace was in ruins. The poets, Rhys Cain and Morus Berwyn, sang the praises of his preaching and noted that he preached in front of the Queen who greatly approved of him.

John Penry would have been glad to know that Morgan encouraged preaching and was meticulous when it came to the standard of preaching within his diocese. During his time at St Asaph, he also repaired the old palace and cathedral. Sir John Wynn writes: 'he repaired and slated the chancel of the Cathedral Church of St. Asaph, which was a great ruin'.

The Legacy

I see Morgan's translation of the Bible into Welsh as:

A return

A belief in God's Holy Word was necessary before there could be any vision of translating it into living languages. The Reformers were returning to the basics: a faith with the Scriptures at its centre. This Bible was not just some moral manual but a map to heaven, an unerring and inerrant revelation, an inspired library compiled over centuries, and an eyewitness account to the wonderful life, death and resurrection of our Lord and Saviour Jesus Christ. This was a return to God's Word.

A rescue mission

That might sound dramatic, but, for Morgan, his translation was part of a spiritual rescue mission. He expressed this in his 1588 dedication:

> *For at that time scarcely any one was able to preach in the British tongue, because the terms in which the sacred mysteries which are in the Holy Scripture should be explained, had either entirely disappeared, swept away as if in Lethian waters, or laid on one side, buried and hidden in a measure in the dust of disuse, so that neither were the teachers able to set forth satisfactorily what they wished to teach, nor the hearers to understand clearly what they did set forth. Besides which so little accustomed were they to the Scriptures, that they were unable to distinguish between the testimony of the Scriptures and their explanation, so much that when they crowded eagerly to hear sermons and paid good heed to them, yet for the most part, they departed in uncertainty and doubt, like men who had found a great treasure which they were not able to dig out, or who had been to a sumptuous feast of which they were not allowed to partake.*

A revival

The translation was part of the Reformation – that locomotive had now reached Wales. She would become a land much favoured by God and her

Bible would be the means by which God would bless this little country again and again in future generations. The use made by Griffith Jones (1684-1761), Llanddowror, of this Welsh Bible in his circulating schools throughout Wales was an important step that boosted the literacy of the people. Next came the great waves of blessing during the eighteenth and nineteenth centuries. These revivals were not driven by emotion, but by God's Word and by his Spirit. Morgan had prepared the ground for these preachers. Then Thomas Charles's endeavours in helping to establish the Bible Society fulfilled Morgan's dream that his countrymen would be able to possess their own copies of God's Word.

The Language

This book needs to conclude with a comment on the Welsh language, a beautiful language which may never have survived were it not for Morgan's work. By updating and improving Salesbury's vocabulary and simplifying the orthography (the spelling system of a language), he was also standardizing the Welsh tongue. He sought to keep some of the oral language of North Wales in the work. Siôn Tudur wrote:

> Iaith rwydd gan athro iddyn'
> A phawb a'i dallt, a phob dyn.

> Clear language, understood by all
> Given by a teacher.

And Rhys Cain:

> Rhoist bob gair mewn cywair call,
> Rhodd Dduw, mor hawdd ei ddeall!

> Every word given in a sensible register,
> God's gift, easily understood!

Morgan used the language of the bards; he showed the wealth of Welsh vocabulary, the agility of its syntax and the precision of its grammatical

65

forms. He introduced a pattern of consistent, standardized Welsh prose which has, overall, survived to this day. This happened at a crucial point in the history of the language because the influence of the bards was rapidly waning. If the Bible had not been translated, Welsh would have disintegrated into numerous dialects which would eventually have been swallowed up by the dominance of English.

He also elevated the status of the Welsh language in the world of learning by opening a door for theological discourse. This was Salesbury's dream: the quest of the Welsh humanist, eventually fulfilled by Bishop Morgan. I like to think of Morgan as a kind of linguistic collector who sought out the best words and recorded them, keeping our language intact to this day.

Death

William Morgan never retired. The main reason for this was that he never reached that old age which we think he did. You would think with that impressive beard that he was at least eighty when he died. Not at all! He died at the age of 59 which, for many of us today, would be considered quite young. The year was 1604, the year that the Hampton Court Conference was held between James I of England, the Anglican bishops, and representatives of the Puritans. This conference put in motion the project that would eventually result in the King James Bible of 1611. I suspect that if Morgan had lived longer, he would have been greatly interested in this venture. He died on 10 September 1604, while John Whitgift died in the February of the same year.

Further quarrels, the most notable being with Sir John Wynn, over local tithes in the diocese, had burdened Morgan's latter days with worry and resulted in his dying as a relatively poor man. The whole of his property at death was valued at £110 1s. 11d. An inventory of his possessions, sold to pay outstanding debts, reveals the extent of his worldly goods:

> *Inventorie of all and singular the goodes and chattells of the Reverend father in God Will'm late Bishopp of St. Asaph that was seized by*

*auctorytie and commission of the Right Ho Thomas erle of Dorsit
lord Treasurer of England to his mats use and for the payment of the
Debtes dewe by the said late Bishopp.*

In the chamber where the Bishopp lay.

Two fether beddes	
One boulster	*Xs*
Two payer of sheets	*Xs*
A white cadowe	*Xs*
A coverlet	*Xs*
A pillow and pillow beere	*XIId*
A curten over the doore	*XId*
A pott	*VIIId*
A lookinge glasse	*XXd*
Two brushes	*Xd*
A… (bedstead)	*IIs VId*
A greate cupborde	*XXXs*
XLIII peeces of pewter of all	
Sortes Seven pottingers two	
Candlesticks	*XXXs IVd*
Fower Andierns	*XId*
Two flagon pottes	*Vd*

*Two ould gownes, three ould cassocks, certen other old appel
of the said Bishopp, -Vli. Fortie tonne of coles. -VIIIi Vs
A ricke of gorse fagottes, -XXVIIIs IIIId
Tenne hennes, -IIIs*

But in the dedication to his Bible, Morgan had meditated on that 'great treasure' which the Welsh would now be able to dig up by means of the translation. He was referring to the parables in Matthew 13 relating to the kingdom of heaven and its immeasurable value. I sometimes think that Morgan himself sold everything for that kingdom. He may have been a bishop but he gave his time, money and life to provide a service that would not only reveal those wonders to himself, but to all his countrymen as well. In that sense he died a wealthy man, for he had stored up for himself real treasure in heaven.

Conclusion: The Library in the Wilderness

I was recently told the story of how the late Gwilym Humphreys, a godly man from North Wales, came to the Wybrnant sometime in the 1980s or 1990s with a group of Sunday School children. It was quite a large group of children and they sat on the grass by the stream listening to what Mr. Humphreys had to say about the Bible and its translator. Before finishing, he paused. He looked at the house and said that it was William Morgan who had made it possible for the Lord Jesus Christ to speak Welsh and, because of him, they could all now listen to Christ's words in their own language and come to know him as their personal Saviour.

I love that thought. That, surely, is the vision that has driven hundreds of Bible translators through the ages. A desire that Jesus Christ their Saviour would be heard in their mother tongue. No venture is more noble!

Tŷ Mawr holds over 200 different translations of the Bible. We have Bibles that were smuggled into Communist countries; miniature Bibles which could be hidden; military Bibles; children's colour Bibles in Arabic; Braille Bibles for those who are blind; audio Bibles; a Bible recovered from Jerusalem during the First World War; strange Bibles which have Masonic symbols on their covers; gang Bibles; Biker Bibles; Church Bibles; School Bibles, etc. The first Bible that was given to the house was the Esperanto version, a designed language which sought to unify all the languages of the world. Thankfully, that aim was never reached, but it did produce a version of the Bible in the process.

Today, languages are continuing to be saved because of Bible translation by organizations such as Wycliffe Bible Translators which are currently working on 2,617 active translations. There are 7,353 languages existing in the world. 698 of these have a complete Bible. One in five people are still waiting for the Bible in their own language.

Tŷ Mawr is a library in the wilderness. It stands as a parable for the position of the Bible in a largely unbelieving world. But it is still possible for millions to hear the 'wonderful works of God' in their own language (see Acts 2:11). This was Morgan's dream. Many have heard about Jesus and many have bowed the knee. But there is still so much more to be done. We look forward to a time when every knee shall bow, and every tongue confess that Jesus is Lord.

Further Reading

Michael Reeves, *The Unquenchable Flame* (Nottingham: IVP 2009).

Eryn White, *The Welsh Bible* (Stroud: Tempus Publishing 2007).

R. T. Edwards, *William Morgan* (Ruthin: John Jones 1968).

Isaac Thomas, 'Translating the Bible' in *A Guide to Welsh Literature c.1530-1700*, (ed.) R. Geraint Gruffydd (Cardiff: University of Wales Press 1997), 154-175.

Glanmor Williams, *Wales and the Reformation* (Cardiff: University of Wales Press 1997).

Engraving by R. Brian Higham
(the author's grandfather – 'Tadcu')